*For some children,
this is the first time they're being
exposed to the concept of autism.*

*By accurately representing autism,
we can challenge incorrect stereotypes
and help the autistic community feel
more loved and accepted.*

*Children should know that autism
is not a disability, but merely
a different way of being.*

*Welcome to honest representation
and kindness.*

Enjoy.

For Eliza, Evan and Reed.

May your stories
inspire the world to have
the courage and the heart
to always be kind.

If you ask me my name,
I will not tell you.

Not because I don't want to,
not because I am shy or stubborn,
but because *I can't*.

I am non-verbal,
which means I communicate
without speaking.

My name is Eliza Hope. I am *autistic!*

Autism is not a disease and there is no cure. It's not contagious, in fact, it's not even a good or a bad thing.

It's just a difference like the color of your hair or your eyes.

You were born *you* and I was born *me*.

When I was two years old my doctor noticed I wasn't developing like most other children.

They used the word *milestones,* as a sort of ruler, to measure how most children grow and learn over time.

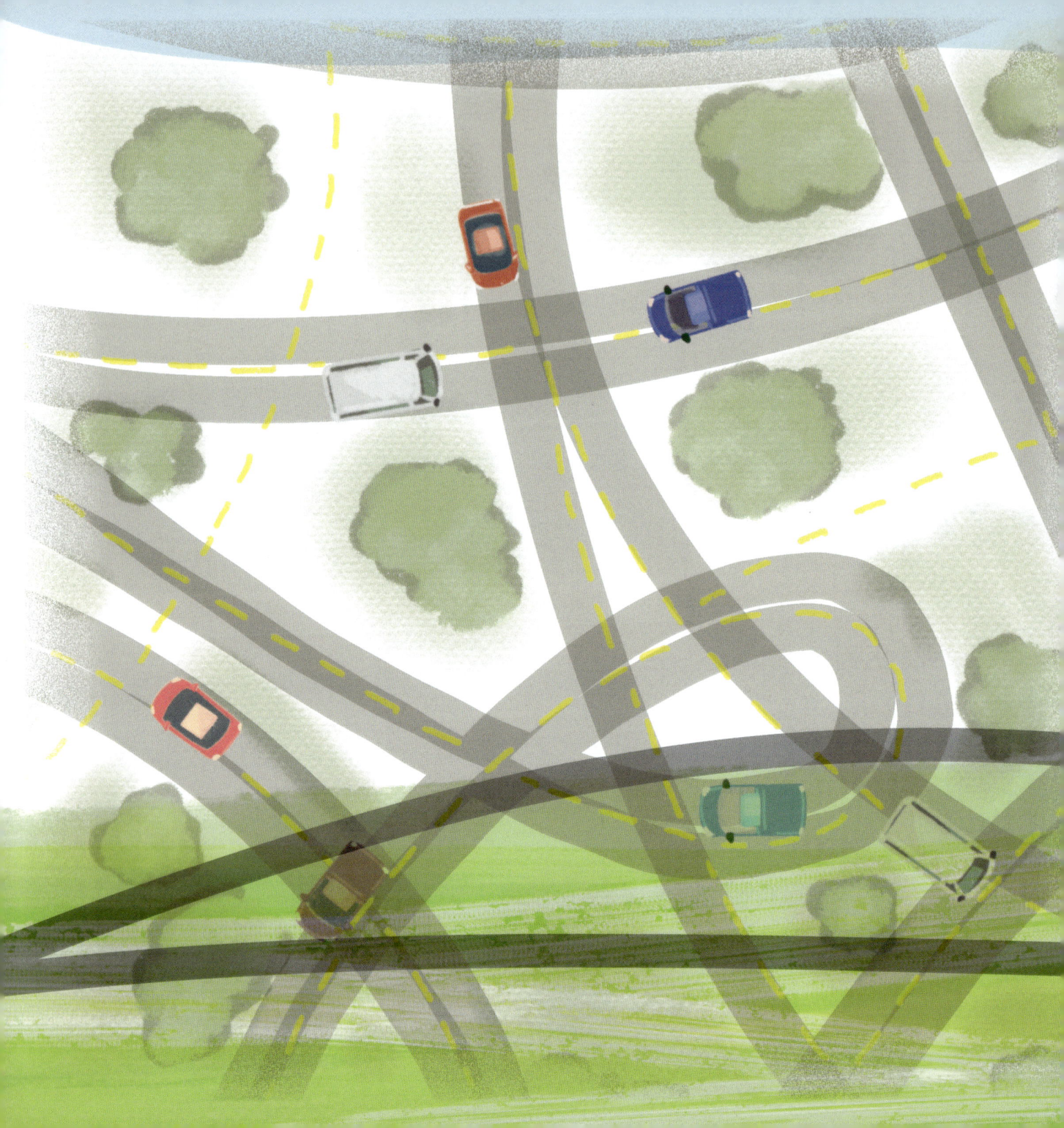

Autism is a brain difference.

Think of your brain as a road with cars driving at different speeds and moving in different directions.

Children with autism might choose to go in the opposite direction to lead them down their own path.

I do not communicate with words. Instead, I sometimes use a tablet to help me express myself.

For example, my tablet has pictures on it of a happy face and a sad face. I can point to either one to show how I am feeling.

Mostly I feel happy.
That button gets pushed a lot!

I can point to my tablet to tell someone when I am hungry and would like to eat.

My favorite food is popcorn.

The popcorn picture on the tablet gets pushed a lot also!

Speaking of favorites,
I love to watch my tv shows and laugh.

I love it when people are kind to me
and say nice things.

On pretty days, I love to go outside and pick up pinecones.

Some people think they are prickly, but I think they are *wonderful*.

Sometimes when I get excited,
I flap my arms up and down
like a butterfly.

That is called stimming,
and there are many different types.

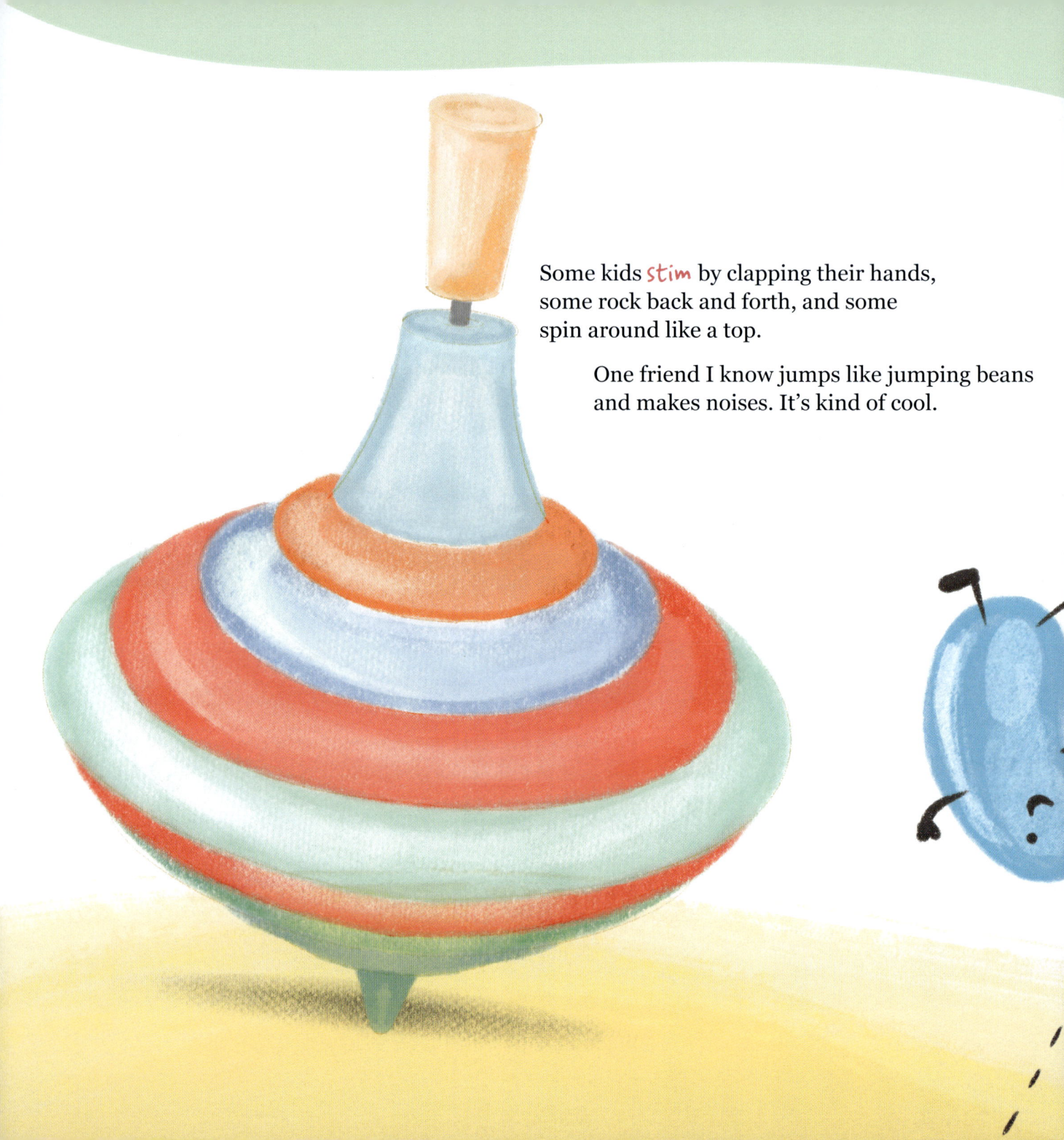

Some kids stim by clapping their hands, some rock back and forth, and some spin around like a top.

One friend I know jumps like jumping beans and makes noises. It's kind of cool.

These movements comfort us and help us release energy from our bodies.

When you see someone stimming, just smile and remember we all express our feelings differently.

Be kind to them.

Sometimes I like to wear my headphones when it's too noisy.

Headphones can also let others know that I might need some quiet time.

When I wear my headphones, *I feel like a superstar.*

All children are *unique* like fingerprints.

So, I guess I am extra *unique!*

The best and smartest people in the world are working on finding out more about autism.

There are also many foundations who are helping provide special services that meet the unique therapeutic and learning needs of autistic children.

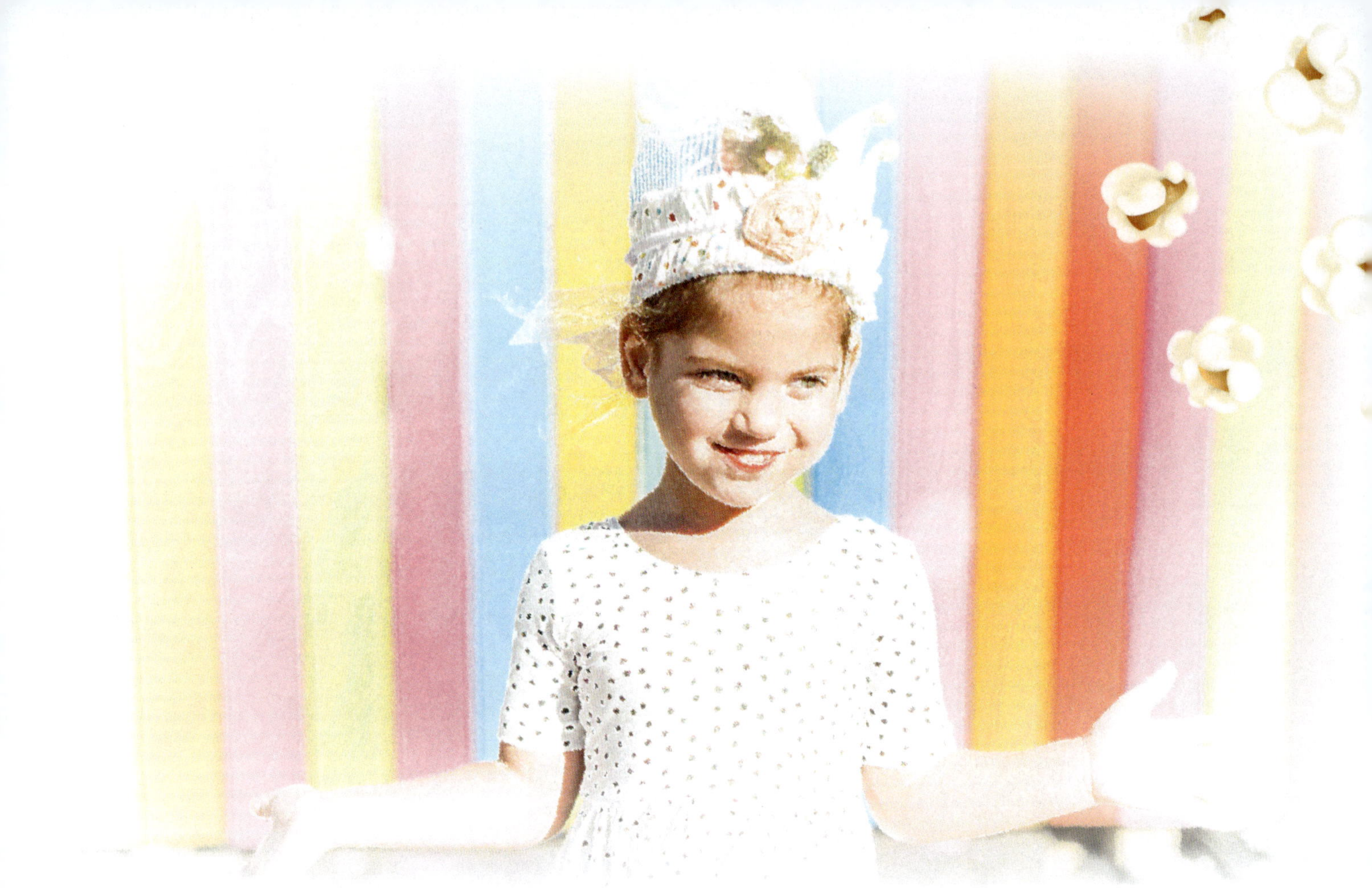

So, next time you think of 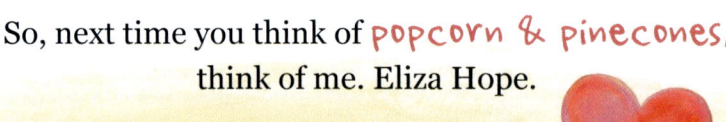, think of me. Eliza Hope.

And always remember to
be kind.

"This is how we choose to honor our daughter, whose life was too short but whose legacy will be remembered forever. This was Eliza's purpose. This was her gift to the world. And, I am just grateful that she was ours." Aimee Darby

www.elizahope.org

*All proceeds from the sales of this book
will be donated to the Eliza Hope Foundation.*

Written by Aimee Darby • Edited by Tammy Deane
Illustrated & designed by Tamara Potter

Copyright © 2024
All rights reserved.
This version printed in 2024.